SHADOWS and MORE SHADOWS

By Illa Podendorf

Illustrations by Darrell Wiskur

 CHILDRENS PRESS, CHICAGO

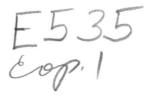

Illa Podendorf, former Chairman of the Science Department of the Laboratory Schools, University of Chicago, has prepared this series of books with emphasis on the processes of science. The content is selected from the main branches of science—biology, physics, and chemistry—but the thrust is on the process skills which are essential in scientific work. Some of the processes emphasized are observing, classifying, communicating, measuring, inferring, and predicting. The treatment is intellectually stimulating which makes it occupy an active part in a child's thinking. This is important in all general education of children.

This book, SHADOWS and MORE SHADOWS, emphasizes observing and inferring, and clearly points up the difference between them.

3 4 5 6 7 8 9 10 11 12 13 14 15 16 17 18 19 20 21 22 23 24 25   R   75 74 73 72 71

CONTENTS

WHOSE SHADOWS ARE THESE?

"Look at my shadow," said Larry.
"I have a shadow, too," said Joe.
"But mine is different than yours,"
said Larry.

"Look at this," said Larry.

"And look at this," said Joe.

"Let's make our shadows alike,"
said Larry.

"We would need to be alike to make
shadows that look alike," said Joe.

Can you see a difference in their
shadows? Look at their hair.

Here are more shadows. How are
they different than those on page 6?
Do they belong to Larry and Joe, too?

Look at these shadows of Larry and
Joe. Are they like those on page 6,
or those on page 7?

Here are three shadows
of Larry.

How could the same boy make such
different shadows? The next page
will give you a hint.

Joe made three different shadows.
He gave each of his shadows a name.

Morning Shadow

Afternoon Shadow

Noon Shadow

11

Are a duck's
shadows
different
at different
times of day?

WHAT MAKES A SHADOW?

There is a morning shadow of a car.
There is the car that makes the shadow.
"There is the sun that gives the light
that causes the car to make the shadow,"
said Larry.

"Ha! There is
a noon shadow.
There is the pole
that makes the
shadow," said Larry.

"There is the
sun that causes
the pole to make
the shadow," said
Joe.

"Once I saw a cloud's shadow from an airplane," said Larry. "It was the sun that caused the cloud to make the shadow."

"Light from the sun,
at any time of day, has
caused all the shadows
we have seen," said Joe.

"Yes. But I can make
shadows in other ways,"
said Larry.

A flashlight will make a shadow.
A lamp will make a shadow.

See this shadow?
The sun made it.

See this shadow?
The flashlight made it.

See this shadow?
A lamp made it.

Will these things make shadows?
They will cast shadows if there
is a light.

If light cannot go through an object, that object will cast a shadow. Things on this page will cast shadows. Light cannot go through them.

WHAT SHAPES ARE SHADOWS?

Larry and Joe cast shadows
that were almost the same shape
they were.

Sometimes their shadows were
longer. They knew this was
because the sun was lower in
the sky at some times.

Larry and Joe might say that
their shadows looked something
like themselves.

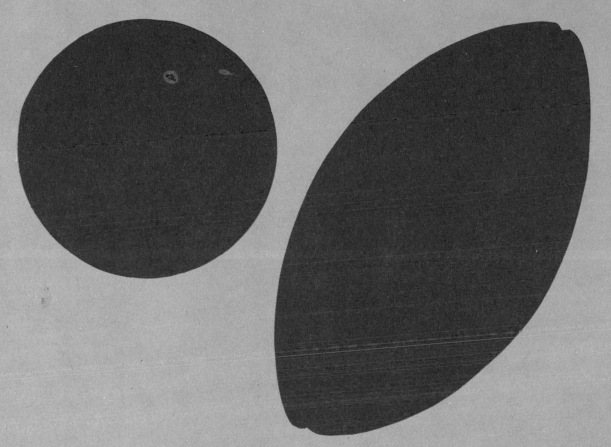

Here are two shadows of the same thing. But the shapes of the shadows are different.

They are shadows of one of the things on page 21. Can you decide which one it is? Did you think it might be the football?

Here are the shapes of three shadows.
One is the shadow of a ball.
One is the shadow of a plate.
One is the shadow of a truck wheel.
Can you tell which is which?
You are sure to say that you
cannot.

Here are other pictures of shadows
of a ball, a plate, and a wheel.
Do they look the same?
Now can you tell which is the
picture of a shadow of a ball, of
a plate, and of a wheel?

Here are more pictures of the shadows of the ball, of the plate, and of the wheel.

The picture of the shadow of the ball looks the same as before.

The pictures of the shadows of the plate and of the wheel look different than the ones on pages 24 and 25.

Here are pictures of three different
shadows of the same object.

Is the object a ball?
A pencil box?
A block?
A can?

Three different shadows of a ball
could be the shape of these pictures.

Three different shadows of a pencil
box could look like these pictures.

Three different shadows of a block
could be the shapes of these pictures.
Three different shadows of a
cylinder-like can would look like
the pictures on page 27.
Did you have that answer?

A can will make other shadow shapes.
Here are pictures of some of them.

Joe is about to spin a top.
Will the shadow spin, too?

Here is the shadow of the spinning
top. You might use your top to see
if the shadow spins, too.

What kind of shadow shapes could this ice-cream cone make?

Could it make one like this?

Or like this?

Could it make one like this?

Or like this?

Here are pictures of two shadows of an ice-cream cone. They are different than those on page 33. Why are they so different?

Here is a picture that tells you
the reason the shadow shapes on page 34
are different than those on page 33.

What kind of a shadow would this flag make?

Could it make one like this?

Or one shaped like this?

36

WHAT MADE THESE SHADOWS?

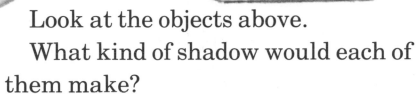

Look at the objects above.
What kind of shadow would each of
them make?

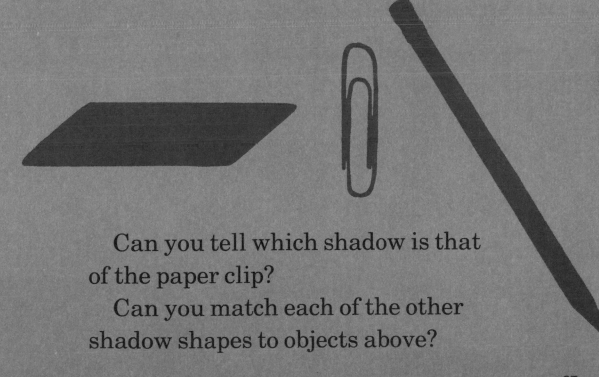

Can you tell which shadow is that
of the paper clip?
Can you match each of the other
shadow shapes to objects above?

Here is the shadow of something
this boy is wearing.
Can you tell what it is?

Can you think of one thing that could
make these different shadow shapes?

This shadow might help you decide what could have made the shadows on page 39.

Look on the next page.

The picture will
tell you whether
your idea was
a good one.

You can see that the pictures of
shadows on these pages are those of
an elephant.

What can you tell about elephants
from the shadow pictures on this page?

What can you infer from this shadow picture?

Here is a kitten playing
with a ball of yarn.

Look at the shadow of the kitten
playing with the ball of yarn.
What has the kitten done?

What does this look like?

Do you think the boy or the rabbit
cast the shadow? Look at the next page.